How to Make an Evacuation Plan

Prepping and Survival Series

M. Usman

Mendon Cottage Books

JD-Biz Publishing

Disclaimer

The information is this book is provided for informational purposes only. It is not intended to be used and medical advice or a substitute for proper medical treatment by a qualified health care provider. The information is believed to be accurate as presented based on research by the author.

The contents have not been evaluated by the U.S. Food and Drug Administration or any other Government or Health Organization and the contents in this book are not to be used to treat cure or prevent disease.

The author or publisher is not responsible for the use or safety of any diet, procedure, or treatment mentioned in this book. The author or publisher is not responsible for errors or omissions that may exist.

Warning

The Book is for informational purposes only and before taking on any diet, treatment, or medical procedure, it is recommended to consult with your primary health care provider.

Our books are available at
1. Amazon.com
2. Barnes and Noble
3. Itunes
4. Kobo
5. Smashwords
6. Google Play Books

Table of Contents

Preface

We are usually clouded with the thinking that disasters happen to other people. Mother Nature can sometimes provide too much of its goodies, resulting in floods and other disasters. Adding to this, accidents can happen at any time necessitating the need to kiss your home goodbye and flee to somewhere safe.

In times like these, your only option is to run. And if you do not have an evacuation plan handy, things can get ugly. Even brain cells you didn't know you had will be bulging against your head, trying to cope with what your eyes and ears are delivering to them.

When the call is made to evacuate, it is impossible to keep one's composure. The least you can do is get your loved ones and run. But, the sad truth is surviving without the basic necessity is impossible. As a matter of fact, you may start wishing you had stayed home.

But, if you were to take the time to prepare for this now, you might be able to survive a scary disaster. In this book, you will learn everything needed to create a perfect evacuation plan. And when the unwanted moment comes, you will have less to worry about.

So, enjoy the reading.

Chapter # 1: Reasons for Evacuation

Despite advancements in every aspect of life, we are still at the mercy of so many disasters. And sadly, not even our brilliant inventions can save us in certain situations. These disasters are man-made and others occur naturally.

It is a pity to hear survivors say they never thought it could happen to them. You should not fall into the same trap. We are all at a risk of facing some disaster every minute we spend on this planet. Here are some examples:

- *Wildfires*: These can start at anytime and anywhere there are trees. A good portion of these are started by humans, but lighting also claims a good percentage. And, if humans are living in its path, an evacuation may be ordered.

- *Floods*: If you do not live under a rock, then you must be aware of increasing flooding incidences. And, as a result, a lot of lives and property have been lost. Partly, global warming is to blame for this.

- *Extreme Cold Weather*: This can be in the form of normal snow or a blizzard. Electricity and water supplies may be cut, making it difficult for people to survive.

- *Extreme Hot Weather*: Being exposed to extremely hot temperatures for too long can kill you. The risk is even higher in the elderly, children, and sick people.

- *Hurricanes*: Statistics show that these have killed about 2 million people over the last 200 years. In 1970, Bangladesh was struck by a cyclone that killed over 300,000 people. But it is not just humans - roads, houses, and other infrastructures can also be destroyed by hurricanes.

- *Volcanic Eruptions*: If you live in what may be a path for a volcano, you might be ordered to evacuate your area.

- *Factory Accidents*: Despite being places which spur development, factories can accidentally release harmful gases. If inhaled, these can have harmful consequences, which is why you might need to leave your home.

- *Terrorism*: The world is not as safe as it used to be. Terrorist are almost everywhere and will kill innocent people just to prove a point or get what they want.

- *Wars*: We are increasingly becoming intolerant of one another, which is why we are seeing a lot of wars all over the world.

The reasons for the need to evacuate are many, and I believe this has opened your eyes to realize that you might not be as safe as you think you are.

Embracing the reality is the best you can do, as you will be prepared for what may fall on you.

Chapter # 2: Know the Possible Dangers

At the heart of every evacuation plan is the knowledge of what could hit you. No one goes to the beach without proper swimwear and the same thing applies here. If you will be making an evacuation plan, you will need to know what you will be running away from. With that, you can decide on the best places to go, mode of transportation, and other important things.

Preparing for a wildfire will certainly differ from a terrorist attack. But still, you will want a plan that covers as many disasters as you possibly can. Here are some ways of knowing disasters likely to happen in your area:

- *Geographic Location*: Most natural disasters do not just happen out of nowhere. Low-lying areas are known for flooding. Volcanoes are common in plate boundaries. As you can see, just knowing this will give you an idea of what to expect.

- *Past Records*: If the area has experienced a certain type of a disaster before, there is nothing stopping it from happening again. Try to find out the frequency at which this has happened.

- **Consult Authorities**: You might end up with more information than you imagined with a simple visit or call to your local authorities. Usually, they monitor any dangers that can harm the population. Another good example is your local Red Cross Society.

- *News*: Whether it is a threat of a war or terrorist attack, watching the news can be very beneficial. Although you might not be exact of when or where it will happen, having an idea is better than being completely blank.

- **Discuss With Family**: One brain is good, two is better. So sit with the family and brainstorm on dangers you may likely face. You might be wowed with what you can accomplish.

Chapter # 3: Be Informed

You do not want to be the last person to know that a disaster is in progress. Hence, the need to stay informed at all times. Usually, the message to evacuate or stay inside will be spread in time for you to take action. But, there are times it happens in an instant, leaving everyone too overwhelmed to respond properly.

Here are some things you should look out for:

- *TV*: Usually, you will get all the information about when to evacuate and places deemed safe from your local TV stations.

- *Radio*: Just like with TV, radio is the other form of communication and probably the most reliable (you can use batteries when there is no electricity).

- *Phones*: You might also get evacuation messages by phone. This might be in the form of calls or text messages.

- *Sirens*: In other areas, sirens are used. This is usually the case with tsunamis. When you hear it, turn the radio on for further information.

- *Door to Door*: People might come to your house and advise you to leave.

There are a lot of ways that can be used to spread evacuation messages. It all depends on the type of disaster and what the authorities think will be the most effective method.

Chapter # 4: Build an Emergency Kit

During an evacuation, time is never on your side. Gathering all the essentials increases the risk of being caught up in the disaster. The same can be said if you are thinking of shopping. But, that does not mean you should just leave home empty handed. You do not want to go hungry or thirsty on the very first day. That is why it is important to have an emergency kit built well before the time.

The people who may save you during a disaster could be in need of saving themselves. So when building your kit, you will want it to be fully equipped with everything crucial for survival. Adding to that, a basic first aid course would also go a long way.

But, let us be honest – building a kit to last even for a week is not easy if you have a big family. Portability is everything in times like these. Fortunately, for the majority of disasters, you might be able to get help in 2 to 3 days. That is why the recommendation is to build a kit that lasts for at least 3 days (the longer, the better). If you find it a little too large, you can separate it into backpacks.

Every member of the house should be able to locate the kit in case a disaster hits when you are away.

With that, let us look at what you will need in your emergency kit:

- *Water*: A healthy adult will only manage to stay alive for 3 days without water. That is why this liquid is among the top three things needed for survival. You should have at least 2 liters of water per person, per day. This will be for drinking and sanitation.

- *Food*: While an average human will still be standing for about 3 weeks without food, including some food will not be a bad idea. Just make sure it is non-perishable. But even then, change it at least twice a year.

- *Sleeping Bags*: This is the closest thing to a bed in the wilderness, and it will keep you warm when cold. Include one for each member of the family.

- *Radio*: It should be battery operated or one with a hand crank. That way, you will stay updated on how the disaster is progressing and any instructions being given.

- *Matches and Lighter*: Fire is important in any survival situation. So, have waterproof matches and a lighter in your emergency kit.

- *Flashlight*: You can include as many as you see necessary. Extra batteries should also be added. To conserve energy, invest in LED flashlights.

- *Map*: This should be of your local area.

- *Cash*: You might need to buy things along the way, stay in a hotel, etc.

- *Whistle*: This will be used to signal for help.

- *Knife*: A knife can be used in a range of tasks including dressing game, building shelter, making weapons, etc.

- *First Aid Kit*: Should include some bandages, gloves, etc.

- *Important Numbers*: These could be of people to stay with or anyone that might help you.

Feel free to add other things you believe your family might not live without (medication). But for the basics, this is all you might need.

Chapter # 5: Communication in Times of Disasters

Communication is the only way we can work together and get things done. And, in times of disasters it becomes even more important. From calling loved ones to know if they are fine to knowing safe routes, its importance can never be overemphasized.

By far, phones are our biggest assets when it comes to one on one communication. You can also use other platforms, such as email, social media, etc. However, for mass communication, nothing beats radio and TV. In the absence of these, the effects of a disaster can be catastrophic.

Here is what you should do:

- *Have a Battery Powered Radio*: It is the most reliable way of knowing how a disaster is progressing. Additionally, authorities will use this to advise the citizenry on what to do. But, since electricity might be out, a battery-operated radio is your best bet. Alternatively, one with a hand crank will also do just fine.

- ***Charge Cell Phones, Laptops and Tablets***: If your cell phone is on, you might call loved ones or text them. But in some situations, cell phones may be rendered useless if the proper infrastructure has been damaged. So, keep your fingers crossed. If network is available, you might also go online for more information. So have your laptop or tablet fully charged.

- ***Have Car Phone Chargers***: Your car will provide an alternative way to charge your phone.

- ***Remove Phone Battery***: This will conserve energy and ensure you have power when you really need to use your phone. Apart from that, you can also close applications you are not using or put the phone in airplane mode.

- ***Have a Non-Cordless Phone***: This works even when there is no electricity. So, having one in your house can prove beneficial.

- ***Keep List of Emergency Numbers***: In the midst of the chaos associated with disasters, you might even forget emergency numbers, despite being easy to remember. But by simply writing them somewhere, you could save yourself from a headache.

- ***Limit Non-Emergency Calls***: During disasters, networks get congested and it becomes difficult to place calls. So if you are thinking of communicating with someone, only call if it is an emergency. Otherwise, use text, social media, or email.

- ***Share Only Important Info***: To avoid the congestion we are talking about, share only vital information when you call someone. You can discuss the rest later when you meet in person.

- **_Wait 10 Seconds before Trying to Call Again_**: If someone did not pick up your call, give it 10 seconds before trying again. You will give them space to return the call that way.

- **_Call Someone Out of Town_**: Placing calls locally is not easy in disasters. So if you need help, consider calling a friend or relative living somewhere else. He or she might be able to call people to help you.

Chapter # 6: Figure out Where to Go

When an evacuation becomes apparent, you do not want to be scrambling at the last minute of where to escape to. This is something to work out in advance. A study showed that during disasters, people will seek shelter where they normally go. Usually, this is at a friend's or relative's house living outside of town. But, not everyone has that opportunity.

Here are some things to consider:

- *Have Multiple Escaping Places*: Since you might never know where the disaster will come from, having a number of places to run to in your evacuation plan is a good idea. If this is a friend's house, have their number handy. You might need to call first, as they could be away from home, etc.

- *Have a Map*: You might need this to figure out routes.

- *Follow Advice*: Usually, the authorities will give advice on the safe places you can escape to. This is typically accompanied with safe routes to use. If you know shortcuts, stay away from them. The roads could be blocked or simply impassable - so you will only endanger yourself.

- *Have Cash*: You might need to stay in a hotel, buy gas along the way, etc. and credit card machines may be down.

Mode of Transportation

While cars are the most convenient form of transportation for ordinary people, in a disaster, they can easily become useless. Roads could be damaged, bridges destroyed, no electricity in pump stations, and more.

Here are some things to remember:

- *Have Another Form of Transportation*: Like stated previously, cars can become useless if roads are destroyed or if there is no gas. So in your evacuation plan, have a contingency mode of transportation.

- *Keep a Full Tank of Gas*: If you know an evacuation is likely, have a full tank of gas. You will be able to get away in time rather than waiting on a pump station or walking on foot. And remember to always have at least a half tank all the time, in case danger strikes without even a warning.

- *Know Alternative Routes*: Knowing other routes will give you the option to use another road when the intended one becomes dangerous.

- *Leave Early*: Since you will not be the only one trying to get away, leave as early as possible to avoid congestion. Not only that, but the roads are also much safer than if you wait till the last minute.

Chapter # 7: Share Responsibility

Working together during a disaster can prove to be a miracle in its own sense. Think about it - you cannot take care of the kids, make calls, and do other important tasks all by yourself. If you were to try, you could do it at the expense of efficiency. Not to mention, you would forget other tasks. So don't try to be a hero – this is no Hollywood movie.

To avoid the situation above, you will have to share responsibility. If there are a couple of grown up individuals in the house, this should not be an issue. You can say A will arrange transportation, B will look after the kids, C will take care of the emergency kit etc.

As you can see, you will get more done. Not only will this ensure successful completion of each task, but you will also have enough time to get away.

Here are things to remember when sharing responsibility:

- *Identify all Needed Skills*: To make it through a disaster, you will need a range of survival skills. For example, injuries can never be ruled out, so ask yourself if there is anyone in the house familiar with first aid. If not, you will need someone on the team with this skill.

- *Assess Individual Skills*: They say everyone is good at something. So, when assigning responsibility, try to match it with the skills of the individual. For instance, if you are not the best driver in the family, give that responsibility to someone good at that.

- *Keep It Simple*: Disasters are stressful situations. Do not build more mountains on the ones you will be facing - make the tasks as simple as possible. If you have no option, divide complex duties into manageable packages.

- *Prioritize*: You might want to take care of everything during a disaster, but time is one mean beast always working against you. To avoid forgoing other important tasks, prioritize. You can do the rest later if you can (closing windows, turning off electrical appliances, etc.). Saving your lives should be the main focus.

- *Practice*: Since practice makes perfect, it makes sense to put your evacuation plan in action every now and then. After all, it is the best way for family members to hone their skills.

- *Remind Each Other*: With time, others may forget their tasks (especially if they start believing a disaster may not happen). This is totally normal. So meet as a team and remind each of the responsibilities. Make everyone realizes they are not different from anyone else - a disaster may strike them at any time.

Chapter # 8: Have a Contingency Plan

If you want to always be successful, always have a plan B. Even better, have a plan C and D, because life never turns out the way you expected. If only we had the power see what the future holds, perhaps it would have been a better story. But sadly, we just have to deal with it.

And when it's disasters in question, the story is the same. Making it worse, is the fact that your life is on the chopping block. And remember, there are no second chances. This is why it is always a good idea to have a contingency plan.

As stated earlier, you should first identify all disasters likely to happen in your area. With that, come up with the best ways of responding to each. Do not expect the disaster to unfold the way you imagined, as you are not the one writing the script. Instead of coming from the south, it may come from the east, etc.

This is where your plan B will come into use. It does not need to be complicated. If you were religious in the previous steps, this stage is simply about asking the question "What if?" For example, what if the order to evacuate comes while you are at work and you have no emergency kit. You can ask yourself as many questions as you see necessary.

Below are some things you should include in your contingency plan:

- *Escape routes*: This is very important, as you will always need a route to escape. So, make sure you are familiar with a couple of roads from all fronts. Having a map is good, but it's even better if you experience the roads physically.

- *Where to Go*: You might think of staying with a friend or relative living out of town. But, what if they too are affected? Having two or more other places to run to will be helpful.

- *Modes of Transportation*: This was said earlier, but it is worth a second mention. Do not build your whole life around a car as the only form of transportation. Think of how you will flee the disaster when it becomes impossible to use a car.

- *Meeting Places*: It is advisable to have a meeting place outside your neighborhood. But, life being what it is, you might not be able to get there. So have second and, preferably, a third meeting place. All family members should be aware of this.

- ***Keep Small Emergency Kit In Your Car***: If for some reason you cannot get home to recover your emergency kit, having one in your car will prove helpful.

- ***Have Other Forms of Communication***: Cellphone batteries may die, electricity might be out, and a whole lot of other unwanted things can happen. Hence, you may need to have another form of communication.

- ***Make Photocopies of Important Documents***: Disasters are known to damage important documents (passports, marriage certificates, bank documents, etc.). If you know it is something you must not lose, make copies of it. Secure these with family members or friends outside of town.

You have the liberty to include other things you deem necessary in your contingency plan.

Chapter # 9: Plan for Your Pets

If you believe you are at the mercy of a disaster, then your pets are equally endangered. If you think they may live without you, you are playing Russian roulette with their lives. It is difficult to stay on top of things when there is an incoming disaster. This is the reason you should plan for your pets now.

If evacuating, it is recommended to bring them with you. Unfortunately, most public shelters do not house pets for health concerns.

Here are things to think about:

- **Ask friends and relatives**: You can make arrangements with a friend living out of area if they could care for your pet. Remember that other homes do not allow animals. So, this is something you should think about in advance.

- **Contact Local Animal Shelters**: In times of emergencies, everyone will think of these places first, resulting in overcrowding. Not to mention that there is inadequate care most of the times. But, if you have no option, anything will do.

- **_Contact Hotels/Motels in Advance_**: Some of these have a no pet policy, but may take pets in times of emergencies. However, you should not assume. A visit or a call is all you need to be sure.

- **_Have Veterinarian Records_**: Since it's a requirement, your pet will surely have these. So, take them with you when evacuating. Officials will ask for them before taking your pet.

- **_Have a Pet Emergency Kit_**: Just like you, your pet will need an emergency kit of his own. It should include food, water, medication, and anything else important for his survival.

- **_Carry Them In a Proper Crate_**: Because of the chaos associated with disasters, your pet may try to run away. This is why you need to keep him in a proper crate. Additionally, you should get him used to being in one so that when the time comes, he will not freak out.

- **_Keep Him in a Room_**: As previously stated, your pet may try to escape, so if you think an evacuation is likely, lock him in a room. When the time to go comes, you will not waste time searching for him.

- **_Have A Recent Photo_**: In case he gets lost, officials will easily identify him if they are clear of how he looks. Remember to bring this photo with you when leaving.

Chapter # 10: Evacuation Plan Template

This chapter will give you an idea of what you may include in your evacuation plan. Before we go any further, know that there is no specific format to follow. As long as it makes sense and it's easy to understand, there is no need to give yourself a headache.

Coming to what you should include, again, there are no rules. If you believe it is necessary, then you have all the good reasons to write it down. The template you will find below is just an example and not something set in stone. Each family is different, and so is every disaster. Do not fear if your plan looks nothing like someone else's.

Since things can get lost, you should have copies kept in several places. That way, you will be guaranteed to never lose it.

Template

Family Evacuation Plan

Family name and Address   Date

Names of Family Members (include all available contacts for each member)

Plan

1. Disasters likely to happen in your area

2. What is the escape plan for each disaster you have listed (include routes, modes of transportation, etc.)

3. Meeting places near your home (If separated, you will first need to meet with family members before leaving. Have two or more of these places near your neighborhood).

4. Emergency contacts (This should include names and contact details of all people you plan to run to. List them in the appropriate order)

5. How will you take care of the elderly or those with special needs? (Include names and a plan for each person)

6. List responsibilities for each family member (Include name, role, and a description of the responsibility)

7. How will you take care of your pets? (Write name, pet license number, color, and any relevant information)

8. How will you meet with children who are in school?

As you can see, the template does not include everything. But, I am sure it has given you an idea of how it should look. And because things change from time to time, keep it updated. At least, aim to do it twice a year.

The most important thing is to practice your plan. That way, it will be much easier to put it into action when the real thing comes. Additionally, you will assess how good each member of the family is at executing their given task. And if there is a need for improvement, you will have all the time to perfect any flaws.

Chapter # 11: Things to Remember Before You Leave

In some situations, you may have time before a disaster hits. In cases like these, it pays to leave your home secured. But mind you, this is only recommended if you have time. Otherwise, reconnect with the family (if separated), get your emergency kit, and hit the road.

Forget about the house, credit cards, and other things you might not need. Your life is far more precious than anything else is. Adding to that, starting out early will guarantee that you avoid the dreadful congestion.

Here is what you should do if you have time:

- **_Turn off Appliances_**: As some might get damaged during the disaster, having electricity running through them will only make things worse. As a matter of fact, your home can literally become a hell on earth. And remember to turn off electricity from the main switch.

- **Turn off Gas**: Gas leakages from damaged pipes are very dangerous. It is even recommended that you call a professional to inspect your home before turning it on.

- **Turn off Water**: With damaged pipes, you can bet you will be fishing your belongings by the time you get back. So turn off water to avoid this.

- **Close Windows**: Others may take advantage of your absence and rob you before they evacuate. So, be sure you have closed all windows. Even better, cover them if you suspect there is going to be a lot of wind.

- **Lock Doors**: Same thing as with windows, you do not want to get robbed.

- **Move All Things Inside**: If there are any items you keep outside, it's best to bring them in before you leave. You could lose them, they could get damaged, or injure someone if not secured.

- **Make Sandbags**: If it is a flood you are running away from, you can keep the water from your house with sandbags. Although not completely effective, trying is better than doing nothing.

- **Cut Overgrown Trees**: During storms, these could fall and damage your house. If you know you have the time, cut these.

- **Make Inventory of Your Home**: In case things have been destroyed or lost, you might need to prove that you are indeed the owner. Having a complete inventory of your house will help in this case. It is recommended that you write everything inside and surrounding your home, but this will take time. Alternatively, you can just make a video recording.

- ***Make Note When Leaving***: Before you leave, you might need to make a note explaining where you will be going. Include the time you left and when you expect to reach your destination

- ***Wear Proper Clothes***: Apart from taking some clothes, you should wear proper ones when leaving. For example, a long sleeve shirt, a pair of trousers and boots will be ideal in most conditions. You will need maximum protection from the cold, mosquitoes, etc.

Conclusion

The basis of this book is how you make an evacuation plan. Just as you read, it is a simple process (Actually, I would jump into freezing waters if you were to sweat with this). It is difficult, if not impossible, to make sound decisions during disasters. Imagine people running all over the place, others screaming, sirens everywhere – it is simply chaotic. And it's understandable for anyone to feel a little hazy. But, when you have a plan in place, things can turn out great.

However, simply making a plan is not enough. You will need to practice it from time to time. Adding to that, things change, so you should keep it updated. Try to involve every member of the house, as you make and update it. That will make it easy for them to adopt it and put it into use.

I hope you enjoyed the book, and remember: You can never be too prepared!

Author Bio

Muhammad Usman is a distinguished medical graduate of Allama Iqbal medical college (AIMC). He is a professional writer who has been in the field for more than 4 years. During this time he has produced 10,000+ articles, blogs, and eBooks on various niches related to diseases, health, fitness, nutrition, and well-being. He is a regular contributor to several journals related to medicine and surgery. He is the editor of several journals and newspapers.

Check out some of the other JD-Biz Publishing books

Gardening Series on Amazon

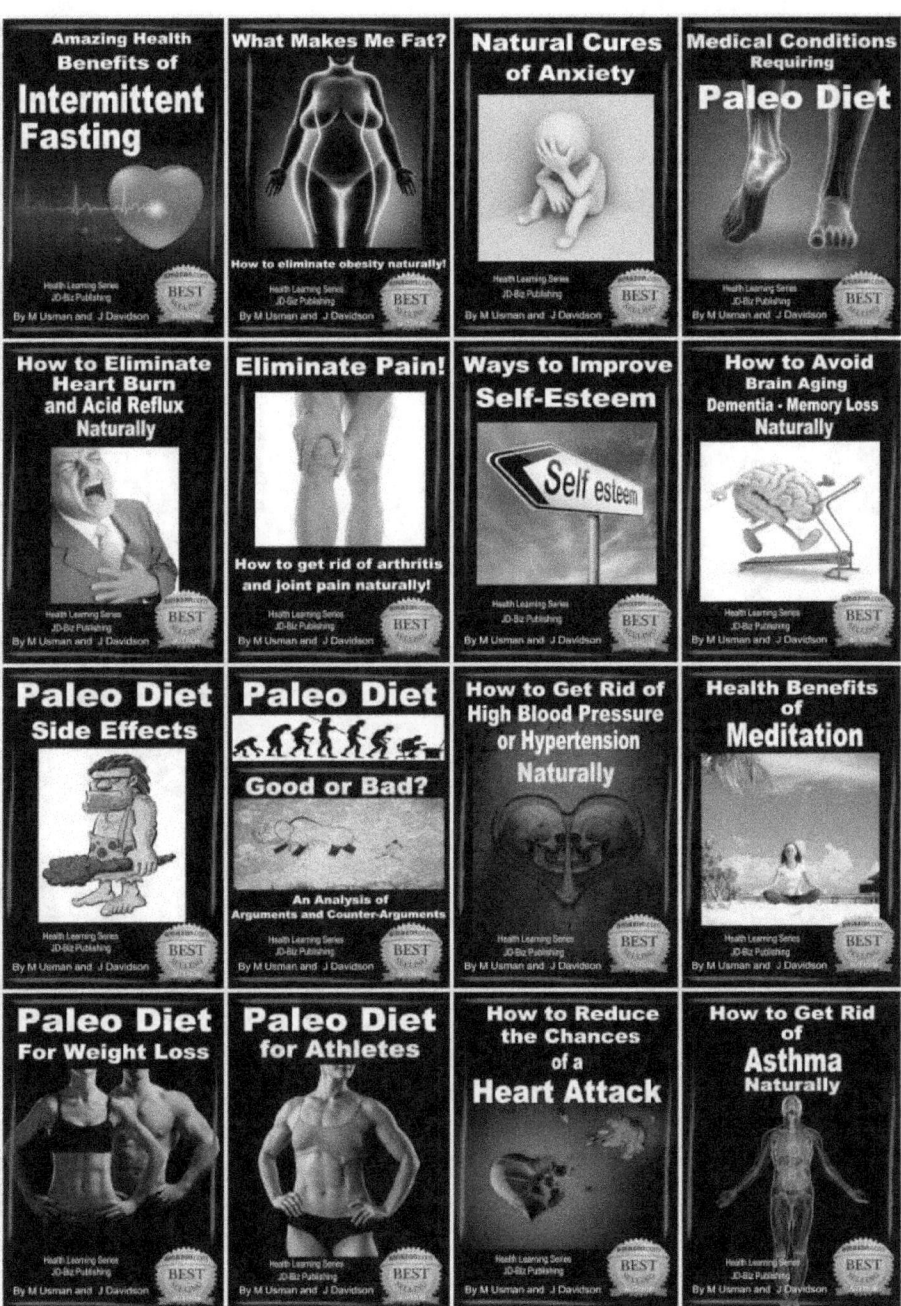

How to Build and Plan Books

Entrepreneur Book Series

Our books are available at

1. Amazon.com

2. Barnes and Noble

3. Itunes

4. Kobo

5. Smashwords

6. Google Play Books

Publisher

JD-Biz Corp

P O Box 374

Mendon, Utah 84325

http://www.jd-biz.com/

Mendon Cottage Books

P O Box 374, Mendon Utah 84325